Marriage in Church after Divorce?

A delicate decison for the clergy

Andrew Cornes

CHRISTIAN FOCUS PUBLICATIONS

By the Same Author
Divorce and Remarriage:
Biblical Principles and Pastoral Practice

ONE2ONE:
Bible Study Material for couples

Copyright © Andrew Cornes 2003

ISBN 1 85792 904 7

Published in 2003
by
Christian Focus Publications
Geanies House,
Fearn, Ross-shire, IV20 1TW, Scotland

www.christianfocus.com

Cover design by
JAC Design, Crowborough

Printed and bound by
JW Arrowsmith, Bristol

In 2002 the General Synod of the Church of England passed a motion about marriage in church after divorce. It began by saying:

'that this Synod affirms in accordance with the doctrine of the Church of England as set out in Canon B30 that marriage should always be undertaken as a "solemn, public and life-long covenant between a man and a woman".'

It went on to:

'Recognize:

i) That some marriages regrettably do fail and that the Church's care for couples in that situation should be of paramount importance; and

ii) That there are exceptional circumstances in which a divorced person may be married in church during the lifetime of a former spouse'.

This motion was certainly not arrived at lightly. But it puts a very heavy weight of responsibility on the shoulders of the parish clergy.

The General Synod, and the House of Bishops, are absolutely clear that the responsibility for deciding whether or not to conduct a second marriage rests entirely with the parish clergy ('second marriage' and 'remarriage' are used throughout this booklet for a marriage where at least one partner is divorced and their divorced spouse is still living). This makes for extremely difficult decisions both about general policy in the parish and about individual cases.

Before 2002, the official position of the Church of England was that there could be no remarriage in church and the large majority of the clergy followed this practice most, or all, of the time.

Now, by contrast, each member of the clergy is largely on his or her own. The House of Bishops has offered advice but has also made it clear that each decision has to be taken by the parish clergy and no-one else.

This booklet aims to help clergy in taking these decisions. It is written in the light of, and in response to, four official documents:

- *Marriage: A teaching document from the House of Bishops* (1999, referred to as *Marriage* in the quotations that follow)
- *Marriage in church after divorce: A discussion document from a Working Party commissioned by the House of Bishops in the Church of England* (2000, referred to as *Marriage in church*)
- *Marriage in church after divorce: General Synod Paper 1449B* (2002, referred to as *Advice to the clergy*)
- *Marriage in church after divorce, Form and Explanatory Statement: A leaflet for enquiring couples* (2003, referred to as *The Application Form*)

NEW TESTAMENT ISSUES

Any serious attempt to formulate and apply a Christian policy about remarriage must begin with the New Testament. *Marriage in church* is very clear about this: 'We regard the close study of the relevant biblical passages in the New Testament as an essential starting point for any consideration of this subject' (p.10).

The teaching of Jesus

There are five passages in which Jesus is recorded as speaking about remarriage. Four of them occur in the Gospels:

- 'I say to you that anyone who divorces his wife, except on the ground of unchastity, causes her to commit adultery; and whoever marries a divorced woman commits adultery' (Matthew 5:32)
- 'I say to you, whoever divorces his wife, except for unchastity, and marries another commits adultery' (Matthew 19:9)
- 'Whoever divorces his wife and marries another commits adultery against her; and if she divorces her husband and marries another, she commits adultery' (Mark 10:11-12)
- 'Anyone who divorces his wife and marries another commits adultery, and whoever marries a woman divorced from her husband commits adultery' (Luke 16:18)

5

To this should be added a fifth passage where St Paul – uncharacteristically, and clearly to bolster the authority of the teaching – quotes or paraphrases the instructions of Jesus while he was on earth:

- 'To the married I give this command – not I but the Lord – that the wife should not separate from her husband; but if she does separate, let her remain unmarried or else be reconciled to her husband; and that the husband should not divorce his wife' (1 Corinthians 7:10-11)

Paul makes it clear that his quotation of Jesus ends at this point because the next verse begins: 'To the rest I say – I and not the Lord - ...' (verse 12).

If, then, we are to take the teaching of Jesus seriously as we weigh up whether to conduct a remarriage, we are bound to be very cautious. Jesus constantly calls remarriage 'adultery'. 'Adultery', in Aramaic, Greek and English, means sexual intercourse where one or both parties are married, and is distinguished from 'fornication' (pre-marital sex) which means intercourse where neither party is married.

If, then, Jesus calls remarriage 'adultery' it is because in his eyes the original marriage still exists. It may have been dissolved in the eyes of the law, it may have come to an end emotionally a long time ago, but the marriage still exists in God's eyes. That is why Jesus can say that remarriage is 'committing adultery *against her* [the first wife]' (Mark 10:11). If the first marriage was dead and gone, it would be impossible to commit adultery against one's first wife. But if the first marriage is still a reality in

6

God's eyes despite the legal divorce, then to remarry is to commit adultery.

People often imagine that the reason why the Churches have historically forbidden remarriage is because divorce is somehow an unforgivable sin. This is of course entirely untrue. Churches have refused remarriage not because one or both of the couple are *divorced*, but because they are *married*. Legally they are divorced; in God's eyes they remain married 'till death us do part'.

This is also why Paul says that after separation/divorce (the words he uses are interchangeable in Greek) a divorcee must remain single or be reconciled to her/his marriage partner (1 Corinthians 7:11). He understands Jesus' teaching to preclude remarriage.

Jesus' words in Matthew certainly contain an exception to his teaching that there is to be no divorce. He allows divorce 'on the ground of unchastity': that is, where one partner has been sexually unfaithful (Matthew 5:32; 19:9)

Does this exception also mean that remarriage is permitted by Jesus where there has been adultery? Scholarly opinion is divided on this issue. Some argue that Jesus allows both divorce and remarriage to the partner whose husband or wife committed adultery. Others argue that divorce alone is permitted.

This booklet is too short to discuss the arguments on both sides. I have done so elsewhere (see the brief bibliography). What is clear, however, is that Jesus was, in general, strongly opposed to remarriage. He consistently called it 'committing adultery'. He never spoke positively of it, only negatively.

The teaching of Paul

Paul is the other New Testament writer who mentions remarriage. In fact, he is not giving new teaching, but merely reiterating – and quoting – the teaching of Jesus.

It is sometimes said that Jesus allowed one exception to his rule of no remarriage (adultery) and Paul added another (desertion on the grounds of spiritual incompatibility).

This is in fact not so. It appears that the Corinthians were asking him whether a Christian ought to divorce his or her non-Christian marriage partner. He first quotes Jesus as saying that Christians should not divorce or remarry (1 Corinthians 7:10-11, quoted above) and then applies this specifically to the situation they have raised: a Christian is not to divorce their pagan marriage partner (verses 12-14).

He does say that the Christian does not have to fight a divorce which the non-christian insists on. The Christian is not 'enslaved' (literally) to the marriage vow, so that he need not at all costs insist on contending the divorce (verse 15). But this is not to say that the Christian can initiate the divorce, still less that he is free to remarry.

In the only clear reference to remarriage after divorce, Paul definitely states that it is not an option for the Christian: 'If she does separate, let her remain unmarried or else be reconciled to her husband' (verse 11). This is in the middle of his quotation of Jesus' teaching.

Exceptional

A 1978 Church of England Report said: 'It is fitting that we should ask first, as of primary importance, what Jesus himself taught about marriage' (*Marriage and the*

Church's Task p.39). If this is so, then for the parish clergy to conduct remarriages must be, at most, exceptional.

All the recent Church of England documents stress this: 'A further marriage after a divorce is an exceptional act' (*Marriage* p.18; *Marriage in church* p.vi). The General Synod motion specifically added (by way of amendment) this same emphasis: 'There are *exceptional* circumstances in which a divorced person may be married in church'.

The Application Form, which the House of Bishops commends to be given to all 'enquiring couples' begins: 'The Church of England teaches that marriage is for life. It also recognizes that some marriages sadly do fail and, if this should happen, it seeks to be available for all involved. The Church accepts that, *in exceptional circumstances*, a divorced person may marry again in church during the lifetime of a former spouse'.

If we are to follow the teaching of Christ, then, we cannot say: 'This Parish Church conducts the remarriage of divorcees'. The basic position must be: 'This Parish Church sadly feels unable to remarry divorcees'. Some churches will believe Christ's teaching allows them occasionally to conduct a remarriage; but if so, it will only be in exceptional circumstances.

PASTORAL ISSUES

While the New Testament teaching must be our primary consideration, and we could never consciously go against the teaching of Christ in the New Testament, there are also pastoral issues to be weighed.

9

1. Consistency

The Bishops' *Advice to the Clergy* states that it is of the utmost importance to treat all cases consistently: 'In deciding your response to [any] application, you need to ensure the maximum degree of consistency in your approach (as applicants are entitled to have their cases dealt with by you consistently) as well as bearing in mind the consequences of setting a precedent which it will be hard not to follow' (p.6).

This is obviously very sensible advice; but it will be extremely hard to put into practice. It is possible to be consistent by saying 'yes' to all enquirers; this, however, is so opposed to New Testament teaching that most clergy will want to reject it.

It is also possible to be consistent by saying 'no' to all enquirers. This, said as gently and sensitively as possible, is what most Anglican clergy have done until now.

It is very hard to be seen to be consistent if we say 'yes' to some and 'no' to others. We may in our own minds be working to utterly consistent principles, but it will rarely appear so to any couple whose marriage we refuse.

2. Clergy as Judge and Jury

The House of Bishops clearly envisages that the parish clergy will take considerable care in establishing the facts in each case and will then decide whether it is appropriate to conduct a remarriage: 'It is your responsibility to form your own judgement as to whether to proceed with the proposed further marriage, in the light of the Church's teaching on marriage [defined in a footnote as Canon B30 and the 1999 Teaching Document *Marriage*] and of the General Synod's Resolution of July 2002' (*Advice to the clergy p.3*)

The Bishops outline 13 searching questions on which 'you may find it helpful ... to satisfy yourself' and these are themselves grouped under 7 further questions:

- Do the applicants have a clear understanding of the meaning and purpose of marriage?
- Do the applicants have a mature view of the circumstances of the breakdown of the previous marriage and are they ready to enter wholeheartedly and responsibly into a new relationship?
- Has there been sufficient healing of the personal and social wounds of marriage breakdown?
- Would the effects of the proposed marriage on individuals, the wider community and the Church be such as to undermine the credibility of the Church's witness to marriage?
- Would permitting the new marriage be tantamount to consecrating an old infidelity?
- Has either of the parties been divorced more than once?
- Do the applicants display a readiness to explore the significance of the Christian faith for their lives so that their further marriage is not an isolated contact with the Church?

(*Advice to the clergy* pp3-4).

The Bishops clearly regard these questions as important and encourage the parish clergy, on the basis of the couple's answers, 'to form your own judgement as to whether to proceed with the proposed further marriage'.

It is precisely this that many clergy are reluctant to do. They feel that it is a flawed exercise because they are only hearing one version of the facts; doubtless the absent divorced partner would tell a quite different story, much less favourable to the couple they are interviewing. Moreover, many parish clergy feel strongly that they can explain and apply the teaching of Jesus, but they cannot be judge and jury about individual cases.

3. Parishioners' anger
When a policy is clear-cut and indiscriminately applied, it is normally accepted even if it is not always understood. Most clergy who have until now followed the Church of England's official teaching and gently refused all requests for remarriage have found that couples have been sad but have usually expected the refusal. They may well only have asked 'because it was worth a try'.

They may not understand, still less agree with, the Church's reasons. But they are aware that the Church stands for life-long marriage and have some idea that the refusal must be connected with that conviction. At any rate, if it is a policy that is applied to all parishioners without exception (even the Churchwarden's daughter), it can be accepted.

But as soon as the church accepts one couple's request and refuses another, there will be a great amount of anger. However much it is clear in the Vicar's mind that he is following consistent and carefully worked out principles, it will never be clear to the couple concerned. They simply will not understand 'why you were willing only last month to marry Jim and Catherine and yet you won't marry us'.

And this anger will not be directed at a distant bishop but at the incumbent who has taken the decision. Nasty letters will be written; there will be hostile telephone calls, during which his most careful explanations will be repudiated out of hand; and poisonous rumours will circulate in the parish.

Marriage in church is greatly underrating the situation when it states: 'Some [incumbents] are undoubtedly reluctant to be drawn into the position of having to discriminate between requests from parishioners' (pp 38-39). They will be even more reluctant when they are exposed to the anger of those whose second marriages they have refused.

4. Clergy feeling exposed

In the original proposals, set out in *Marriage in church*, the incumbent was to be supported in every case by his or her Bishop. 'Without proposing any transfer from incumbents of the decision whether or not to marry, we nevertheless judge that as a matter of good practice they should be required to seek outside advice ... We recommend that incumbents refer all cases to their diocesan bishop with his role being to see that the right procedures have been followed, to offer whatever pastoral guidance he might feel appropriate, and to be available for consultation in difficult cases' (p.39).

To some degree, then, the incumbent had the support and backup of his Bishop in every case.

The House of Bishops has now changed its mind on this: 'On reflection, we believe that such reference [of all cases to the diocesan bishop] should be possible but not obligatory' (*Marriage in church after divorce: A report from the House of Bishops [GS 1449]* p.6)

In the Bishops' *Advice to the clergy*, they do continue to offer their advice when asked for. But this is hedged about: 'It should be noted that bishops cannot give permission for couples to be married in church and that applicants should not approach the bishop direct' (p.6).

Moreover, the correspondence between incumbent and bishop cannot be confidential. The incumbent, when seeking advice, is to send the Bishop various pieces of information 'including any provisional conclusions you have reached'; but 'you will need to bear in mind that the couple will be entitled to see what you have written (under the Data Protection Act)' (p.6). 'You should write your notes, your recommendation and your correspondence with the bishop in a way that can readily be shared with the couple' (p.8).

This leaves the clergy feeling very exposed in decisions which may have significant repercussions in the parish.

5. Clergy time

The Bishops' *Advice to the clergy* rightly recognizes that each case will need to be carefully and sensitively looked into before a considered judgement can be reached about whether a remarriage would be appropriate: 'If the couple's request is to be taken further, the background of their case needs to be explored very carefully ... Both partners should attend the interviews, having been made aware in advance of the searching and personal nature of the issues to be discussed' (p.5).

The Bishops recommend in each case 'at least two confidential interviews' before any decision is taken (p.5). *The Application Form* says to the enquiring couple: 'This process [of deciding about a possible remarriage in church] could easily take some time, and you should discuss how long it might take with your parish priest at your initial meeting'.

If the incumbent takes the decision to conduct the remarriage, further meetings will be necessary for marriage preparation: 'In cases where you agree to the couple's request, you will need to explain the need for marriage preparation (as for any marriage)' (p.6).

If the incumbent takes the decision to refuse the request for remarriage, he is expected to write on the Application Form his 'grounds for refusing the application' and then to sign the form. This material will certainly be available for the couple to see.

The grounds for refusal will anyway need to be communicated to the couple: 'It will be best if you convey your decision to the couple in person. If you are declining to conduct the marriage, you may feel it appropriate to convey your reasons in writing' (p.6).

Refusal to agree to conduct a remarriage, in a parish where some second marriages in church do take place, will very likely result in further meetings not only with the couple themselves but with irate members of their family and friends.

It is obvious that this issue of remarriage could take up an immense amount of clergy time.

6. Pressure to accept all applications

Nobody likes being the butt of anger; and in the face of anger the temptation is always strong to back down.

Marriage in church rightly states: 'In considering what course to adopt, you [the incumbent] should always bear in mind the consequences of setting a precedent which it will be hard not to follow' (p.57). This sentence was probably included to help incumbents to take the difficult course of refusing applications; it shows, however, that the more applications for remarriage an incumbent accepts, the harder it will be for him or her to refuse the next application.

When people are angry, they tend to speak to their friends and neighbours. Soon an incumbent's name, and the name of the parish church, will be besmirched in the community. The incumbent's integrity will be called into question, and hostile rumours (many of them untrue) will begin to circulate about him.

In these circumstances, the pressure to cut short the interview process and to accept all applications will become, for many, unbearable. And this pressure will not only come from the wider community and the incumbent's own hurt feelings. Churchwardens and other congregation members may put pressure on the incumbent to relax his policy because of the bad feeling in the town or village, and it will probably not be long before Parish Profiles state that the Church Council is looking for an incumbent who will remarry divorcees.

This process has clearly happened already in other denominations and *Marriage in church* is disarmingly honest about it.

In 1946 the Methodist Conference allowed remarriage for the innocent party in a case of adultery. 'This procedure ... was originally designed for relatively rare cases' (*Marriage in church* p.31). But by 1996, 62% of all marriages in Methodist churches involved at least one divorced person (p.31).

In 1998 the Methodist Conference adopted a report which included a provision that 'normally a minister will honour the couple's request [for remarriage], if made with understanding and faith, to participate in a marriage service in a Methodist church' (pp. 31-32). The 'rare case' has become the norm.

Exactly the same process has taken place in the Anglican Church in the United States, where I served for some years. It too began by allowing remarriage in some circumstances but now agrees to a second marriage in almost every case; in fact, the idea of refusing a request rarely crosses any incumbent's mind.

THE WAY AHEAD

All this presents the clergy with a very difficult dilemma. The teaching of Jesus, and of the New Testament generally, is overwhelmingly opposed to remarriage. It either forbids remarriage altogether or allows it only in exceptional circumstances. Clearly this teaching must be of paramount importance in seeking to establish a policy for the parish and our actual practice in specific cases.

Pastoral considerations show that it is extremely difficult to accept some requests and not others. Even if we think we are following clear and consistent principles, it will almost certainly not seem so to others, particularly the couples we refuse and their friends.

So what are we to do?

1. A policy of no remarriage in church
The only way to be clearly consistent is to have a policy either of accepting all applications for remarriage or gently but definitely refusing all applications.

The former policy is one which Anglican churches will probably increasingly adopt as the years go by. But it simply cannot be squared with the teaching of Jesus. And it is certainly not the way any of the recent Church of England reports want the Church to go. The House of Bishops made its recommendations on the explicit understanding 'that further marriage after a divorce is an exceptional act ... To marry all comers in such circumstances – as some have argued – would open the Church to the accusation that it has abandoned its principles' (*Marriage in church after divorce: A report from the House of Bishops [GS 1449]* p.3).

The other policy – of not allowing any remarriage to take place in church – is much nearer to the teaching of Jesus, who consistently called remarriage 'adultery' and never spoke of it positively. It also has the merit of being an utterly consistent policy which everyone can see is practised indiscriminately.

It will be important for an incumbent to establish this practice at the outset of his or her ministry in a new parish. I had been only a few days in my United States parish when I received a request for a second marriage. It was a delicate situation as it came from a regular member of the congregation. Being new to the States, I immediately asked my Bishop's advice. He was categorical: 'You must start as you intend to go on'. It was good advice.

Of course if an incumbent has on some occasions conducted a second marriage and then becomes convinced – on theological or pastoral grounds – that he would do better to have a policy of no remarriage in church, he will want to follow his conscience. He will then need to explain his new policy to the Church Council and to individuals and couples who may question him. This will have to be faced, but it underlines the point that it is better to start with a policy of no remarriage in church from the outset of a new parish ministry.

My experience is that such a policy, if consistently applied, may not be fully understood or agreed with, but is respected by church members and normally accepted by those couples who request remarriage.

2. Services of Prayer and Dedication

In 1985 the House of Bishops approved a Service of Prayer and Dedication after a civil marriage. This is not a marriage service, vows are not taken though they are reaffirmed, and rings are not given and received, though they may be blessed.

Some clergy will feel this is an appropriate compromise. They cannot, in deference to Christ, conduct a marriage after divorce. But once the civil marriage has taken place, they can offer prayers that this marriage will succeed and will bring joy to the couple, their family and friends. Statistics show that second marriages are considerably more likely to fail than first marriages, and this new marriage will need all the support – including spiritual support – that we can give.

Other clergy will feel that their conscience will not allow them to use this service where there has been a divorce. They agree with the Methodist Church whose position is: 'If a request for a marriage in church is declined, it is deemed inappropriate for the Minister to recommend a civil marriage in a Register Office followed immediately by a service of blessing in a church, on the grounds that whatever reasons ruled out the former would apply theologically to the latter' (*Marriage in church* p.32).

3. Pastoral care of the divorced

The 2002 General Synod resolution began by stating that 'marriage should always be undertaken as a solemn, public and life-long covenant between a man and a woman'. Its next statement was to 'recognize that some marriages regrettably do fail and that the Church's care for couples in that situation should be of paramount importance'.

The churches in this country need to take that statement seriously. We should be putting our energy and resources into caring pastorally for those whose lives have been devastated by marriage breakdown and divorce.

This is undoubtedly the biggest pastoral concern in Britain today. 41% of all marriages will end in divorce. Every year of the last decade between 150,000 and 176,000 children experienced the divorce of their parents. Shock, bewilderment, anger and chronic suffering are experienced not only by the couple themselves and their children but by many members of their family, their colleagues and their friends.

If we are to prove true to the teaching of Christ, we will not only stand up for his understanding of the permanence of marriage (and therefore gently refuse requests for remarriage) but also care for the broken-hearted.

He applied to himself the words of Isaiah:

> 'The Spirit of the Lord God is upon me,
> because the Lord has anointed me;
> he has sent me to bring good news to the oppressed,
> to bind up the broken-hearted,
> to proclaim liberty to the captives,
> and release to the prisoners;
> to proclaim the year of the Lord's favour'
> (Isaiah 61:1-2)

In doing so, he not only set an agenda for himself but for us his followers. If we are to be at the forefront of 'binding up the broken-hearted', we must be involved in pastoral care of the divorced.

It is often imagined that a second marriage will provide precisely this binding up of broken hearts. This can of course sometimes be the case. But the statistics are not encouraging: for example, the marriages of divorced men marrying before the age of 40 are 58% more likely to end in divorce than those of men marrying for the first time; for divorced women the figure is 81%. Moreover, even where a second marriage works reasonably well, the children often resent the intruder into their family and long for the restoration of the original marriage. A new marriage, rather than meeting the children's needs, very often makes their problems considerably worse.

The Christian Church must in any case ask what Christ means by 'binding up the broken-hearted'. His explicit teaching makes it clear that he is not envisaging second marriages for the divorced. Rather, he directs his followers to care for the divorced in the brokenness of their marriages.

This of course also involves time and the clergy may well feel they are very hard pressed already. Lay involvement will almost certainly be necessary.

There are now a number of Church-based groups and organizations caring for the separated and divorced. One such is the Aquila Care Trust. This began in 1991 as a group of Christian divorcees met together to talk and share their experiences, their hopes and their hurts.

So began an eight-week self-help course, covering the multiple problems – emotional, financial, educational, physical and spiritual – that the separated and divorced face. It was initially for divorced church members but rapidly changed to support divorcees in the wider community.

Aquila now helps to set up similar courses all over the country. It is often first approached by church leaders wanting to care for the divorced in their church and secular community. It helps to identify those lay (usually) leaders who could run the course, trains them and continues to support them with course materials, regular newsletters and further training events in different parts of the country.

It has been recognized by the British Government as one of the most significant providers of pastoral care for the divorced. Further information can be had from the Aquila Office:

Tel: 01892 665524;

e-mail: admin@aquilatrust.org;

Web: www.aquilatrust.org.

In the second half of the twentieth century the Church was in the vanguard of pastoral care for the dying through the Hospice movement. In the twenty first century the churches must equally take the lead in caring for the divorced. At the moment, no other organization is offering this care in any systematic or widespread way. It is imperative, therefore, that the churches grasp the opportunity to meet such massive human need in the name of Christ: for forgiveness, healing and gradually regained wholeness.

The Church has the resources for this in Christ and Christian faith; it must help broken people and families to find it.

BRIEF BIBLIOGRAPHY

This bibliography consists only of books cited or alluded to in the text. For a fuller bibliography, see my earlier book *Divorce and Remarriage – Biblical Principle and Pastoral Practice.*

Marriage – A teaching document from the House of Bishops of the Church of England. London: Church House Publishing, 1999.

Marriage and the Church's Task – The Report of the General Synod Marriage Commission. London: CIO, 1978.

Marriage in church after divorce - A discussion document from a Working Party commissioned by the House of Bishops of the Church of England. London: Church House Publishing, 2000.

Marriage in Church after Divorce – A report from the House of Bishops (GS 1449). London: General Synod, 2002.

Marriage in Church after Divorce – Advice to the clergy from the House of Bishops (GS 1449B). London: General Synod, 2002.

Marriage in church after divorce: Form and explanatory statement – A leaflet for enquiring couples. London: Church House Publishing, 2003.

Cornes, A.C.J. *Divorce and Remarriage – Biblical Principle and Pastoral Practice.* Fearn, Scotland: Mentor, 2002[2]

Cornes, A.C.J. *Questions about divorce and remarriage.* London: Monarch, 1998.

Christian Focus Publications

publishes books for all ages.

Books in our adult range are published in three imprints. *Christian Focus* contains popular works including biographies, commentaries, basic doctrine, and Christian living. Our children's books are also published in this imprint.

Mentor focuses on books written at a level suitable for Bible College and seminary students, pastors, and other serious readers. The imprint includes commentaries, doctrinal studies, examination of current issues, and church history.

Christian Heritage contains classic writings from the past.

Christian Focus Publications, Ltd
Geanies House, Fearn,
Ross-shire, IV20 1TW, Scotland, United Kingdom
info@christianfocus.com

For details of our titles visit us on our website
www.christianfocus.com

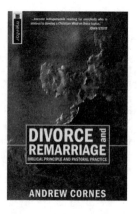

Also by the Same Author:
Divorce and Remarriage:
Biblical Principles and Pastoral Practice

'..indispensable reading for everybody who is anxious to develop a Christian mind on these topics'

John Stott

ISBN 1 85792 756 7
Mentor